Higher

GCSE german for OCR

Exam Skills Workbook

Clare Parker

OCR
RECOGNISING ACHIEVEMENT
OXFORD
UNIVERSITY PRESS
— Official Publisher Partnership —

OxBox

Contents

Contents of CD-ROM

Audio tracks

- Audio tracks from Pronunciation section
- Audio tracks from Listening practice section

Answers

- Answers to Listening practice section
- Answers to Vocabulary in practice section
- Answers to Worksheets section

Preparing for your GCSE

How to get an A*

1 Be organised
- Start preparing as early as possible – don't leave it until the last minute!
- Get to know your coursebook! It contains lots of useful information, so make sure you know where everything is.
- Make sure you know what you will be expected to do in the exams and controlled assessments. This guide is an excellent starting point.

2 Know your vocabulary
- The easiest way to do better in the exams is to learn more words! Learning is a very individual process: try some of the techniques listed below as you work through the course and find out what works best for you.
  - Build up your vocabulary. Have a vocab book or file ready and organise it by topic or alphabetically – whichever grouping you find most helpful.
  - Test yourself. Use index cards and put English on one side and German on the other. Keep practising until you can remember them all.
  - Stick vocabulary notes on your wall and around the mirror so that you see them every time you pass.
  - Little and often is the key to vocabulary learning. Five minutes every day is much better than three hours in one go.
  - Work through the vocab building section of this book (pages 17–23).

3 Know your grammar
- Grammar is the key both to understanding German and to sounding convincing when you speak it! Make sure you have a firm grasp of the basics so that you use the right person (e.g. *du* or *Sie*) and talk about actions in different tenses.
- Make sure you can give opinions, describe things and link sentences.
- Work through the 'Aktive Grammatik' pages in each unit of the coursebook and the grammar bank at the end of the book. Ask your teacher if there is something you need additional clarification on.
- Get extra practice. Work through the grammar activities in this book. The *GCSE German for OCR Grammar Workbook*, too, provides lots of additional practice material to help you consolidate your grammatical knowledge and skills.

4 In your spare time
- Listen to German as often as you can: you can listen to German radio stations and watch some German TV programmes online, and DVDs of German films are also readily available. Try listening to a movie with German sound but English subtitles – it's great comprehension practice!
- Exploit the Internet. Why not search for German-language editions of your favourite websites or read some German magazines online?

5 Before the exam
- Be organised. Have a revision timetable planned out well in advance so that you leave enough time to get through everything.
- Revise your German often, linking your practice to different tasks to keep it interesting for you.
- Make sure you know what is expected of you. Four different skills are examined: *listening, reading, writing* and *speaking*. Listening and reading are assessed in sit-down exams, but speaking and writing are tested in controlled assessments. Consult the speaking and writing sections of this book for examples of the kind of tasks you will do in them.

Preparing for the listening exam

In the listening exam, you will be given five minutes' preparation time in which to read the question paper before the recording is played. The listening material lasts up to 45 minutes. You will hear each item twice.

There will be five tasks on the paper. All the instructions will be given in English.

Some of the questions will be multiple choice and some will require you to write short answers in English.

The recorded material will consist of messages, announcements, monologues, dialogues and discussions of varying length. Recorded instructions will be given at the beginning.

1 Before the exam
- Make sure you are confident with the German sound–spelling system (you can revise this using the pronunciation guides on the *GCSE German for OCR OxBox CD-ROM*).
- Listen to German as often as possible: to music, films, radio, even German television (if you can access it via cable TV or online) and, of course, the CDs that accompany this course.
- Invent your own shorthand so that you can take notes quickly.
- Prepare for the different types of question. Make a list of the different types of question used in the sample assessment material in this guide.

2 At the start of the exam
- Before listening, use your five minutes of reading time carefully.
- Predict the context of each question. Look for background information from the title, introduction and picture (if there is one). Start to think about the type of vocabulary and phrases you are likely to hear.
- Read the questions carefully. They will all be in English and the questions will often contain valuable clues.
- Make sure you are doing exactly what is required in order to answer the question. If it is asking for details, then listen out for key words. If it is asking for an overall impression, then try to sum up the information required.

3 While the recording is playing
- Remember that you will hear everything twice and you should have plenty of time to write down your answers.
- Listen to the tone of voice and the intonation of the speakers. This can sometimes provide useful clues as to a speaker's opinion.
- Listen for the verbs, tenses, number and gender of nouns. All of these can help you decipher the precise meaning of what is being said.
- On the first listening, listen for the gist, or general sense, of the passage; on the second, listen out for the required details.
- Make short notes. You needn't write full sentences for your answers unless specifically asked to do so.
- You may be helped by words that sound like English words in the recording, but be aware of false friends (see page 7)!
- Don't panic if you don't understand everything. Often it is not necessary to do so. Concentrate on what you *do* understand.

4 **After the recording has stopped**
- Check what you have written. It's easy to make a slip when you are writing quickly, so check that your answers make sense.
- Don't leave any blanks. You might pick up some valuable marks, even if you are unable to give all of the information required in an answer.
- If you are not sure of the answer, make a sensible guess, using what you know about the context of the question, about German-speaking countries in general, and your knowledge of the German language.

Preparing for the speaking controlled assessment

Your speaking skills will be assessed in a controlled assessment. This means that you will prepare for a speaking task under exam conditions and then present your work to your teacher, language assistant or examiner either on an individual basis or in a group. The final task might not take place in a classroom: it just needs to take place in a situation in which the assessor can judge how well you do it.

For your speaking assessment, you need to be able to:
- Communicate on one or more topics for two different purposes. The topics can be selected from OCR's list, or your teacher might choose a different suitable task for you.
- Interact with other speakers and present ideas and information.

This means that you must do two tasks of the following types:
- a presentation
- a role play
- a conversation

from the following topic list:
- home and local area
- health and sport
- leisure and entertainment
- travel and the wider world
- education and work

or from any other suitable topic area.

1 **Before the controlled assessment**
- Practise speaking German as often as you can, with a friend, a classmate or even by yourself.
- Be a copycat! Try to imitate your teacher's accent or that of the German speakers you hear in recordings and videos. Use the pronunciation guide on the OxBox CD-ROM to help you to sound more authentic and convincing.
- You can practise different types of conversation, presentation and role play in class with your teacher and your classmates and your teacher can offer you advice and tips.

2 **Preparing the task**
After finding out what each speaking task is, you will have two hours in which to prepare for it. The two tasks might not take place at the same time.

During the preparation time, you may:

- Consult reference materials such as dictionaries, Internet resources and coursebooks, in order to find out any information, words or phrases you need.
- Make **notes** or prepare a **visual stimulus** to use when you present the task:
  - Notes should contain no more than 40 words: five bullet points with no more than eight words per bullet point, but this may include conjugated verbs.
  - Notes must be written on a special form that OCR provides. This form is submitted with work for assessment.
  - A visual stimulus is a picture, such as a photograph, that does not display any words or symbols.

You may discuss with your teacher:

- the type of task and what you are expected to do
- how to use reference material
- how to prepare the notes or the visual stimulus.

You may not ask your teacher:

- for words and phrases in German to be included in your work
- to comment on or correct your notes
- to practise the task with you
- to practise recording the task with you.

3 Performing the task

- You have between four and six minutes to complete each task.
- Speaking tasks may be carried out in any appropriate location as long as they are supervised. They may take place in the classroom or any other part of the school. They may even take place outside the school, for example on a school visit.
- Your teacher, a teaching assistant or a language assistant will supervise you during the final task.
- You are allowed to refer to your notes, the speaking information form describing the task and the visual stimulus you have prepared.
- You are not allowed to use a dictionary.
- You will not be given any feedback or assistance while you are conducting the task.

The two tasks will each be marked as follows:

Communication:	15 marks
Quality of language:	10 marks
Pronunciation and intonation:	5 marks
Total:	**30 marks (x 2 tasks)**
GRAND TOTAL:	**60 marks**

Preparing for the reading exam

1 Before the exam

- Making note of new words you meet in written texts will help your reading comprehension skills. The more words you recognise and understand, the more you will be able to get out of a text.
- Try to read German as often as possible. Your teacher may have magazines you can borrow, but why not search for German-language websites on topics that interest you? Using a German search engine, such as **www.google.de**, with German search terms will enable you to find them easily. Try to understand as much as you can. Discuss what you have read with friends and teachers and make a note of new vocabulary. This will help the new words you meet 'stick'.

2 During the exam

- The higher exam lasts for 45 minutes.
- Watch your timing carefully. You do not want to be rushing to finish at the end.
- Try to predict the contents of what you are about to read: pictures and titles can provide valuable contextual clues and enable you to make more accurate guesses about sections you don't understand.
- Read the question closely and make sure that you know what you are being asked to do. Check the examples carefully to make sure you understand the task.
- Read the questions first and *then* the text. Concentrate on the information you need and ignore everything else.
- If you get stuck on one question, leave it and go on to the next question. This will help save valuable time and give your brain a chance to process the information. Just make sure you don't forget to go back and look at it again later!
- Try to work out the meaning of unfamiliar words. The following strategies can help:
  - Look for German words that are similar to English ones, e.g.
    Freund = friend
  - Look for relationships between German words, e.g.
    freundlich − Freund − Freundschaft
  - Beware of false friends, e.g.
    Gymnasium = grammar school (not a gymnasium)
    bekommen = to get, to receive (not to become)
  - Use your knowledge of grammar:
    If you see a word that looks related to a word you know, it could, for example, be a different tense of a verb you know.
    If a word is totally unfamiliar, but you can tell that it is a verb because of its position and function in the sentence, can you work out what tense it is in? This could help you answer the question.
    Make sure you have correctly identified the subject of the sentence. Articles and endings will help you to do this.
- You needn't answer questions with full sentences unless you are asked to do so. This could save valuable time.
- All questions on the exam paper will be in English and should be answered in English, except for one question which will require a non-verbal answer in German.

3 After the exam

- Leave enough time at the end of the examination to read through your paper. Check that you have not missed any questions out and make sure that you have written an answer for each one. As with listening, if you do not know an answer for certain, then make an educated guess. Do not leave any blanks. You never know − your lucky guess could be right!

Preparing for the writing controlled assessment

Your writing skills, like your speaking skills, will be assessed by controlled assessment rather than by examination. Two tasks will be set by your teacher and completed under exam-like conditions, but not necessarily in an examination hall. You will have time to prepare for the tasks in advance, using reference materials.

You will submit both pieces of written work for assessment.

1 Before the controlled assessment

- When writing it is particularly important to be sure of the genders and spellings of the words you want to use. Make sure you revise these before the assessment.
- This is your opportunity to show what you can do when writing in German and that you can approach the task at your own level.
- Ask your teacher to show you the mark scheme so that you know what is required in order to obtain particular grades.
- To gain the highest grades, you will need to be able to express your opinions in a variety of different ways. Try to learn and use as many of the following expressions as possible:
  Ich mag
  Ich mag nicht
  Ich finde ... gut/schlecht
  Ich glaube, dass ...

Don't forget to justify your opinions as well:
..., weil ... — because
..., da ... — as, since

- You will need to use a variety of tenses, past, present, future and conditional:
  Ich gehe gern ... — I like to go
  Ich habe ... gemacht — I have done
  Ich bin ... gefahren — I went
  Ich werde ... studieren — I will study
  Ich möchte ... machen — I would like to do

Try to learn these phrases so that you can adapt them where necessary.

- It would also be good if you could use some imperfect verb forms, such as *ich hatte* and *ich war*.
- Modal verbs are also very useful additions to your written work:
  Ich kann — I can
  Ich muss — I must

Don't forget to put the infinitive at the end of the sentence or clause after a modal verb:
*Ich **kann** nach der Schule **kommen**.* I can come after school.

- Modals are also useful in the imperfect:
  Ich wollte — I wanted
  Ich konnte — I could
- Try and use the *er* and *sie* forms and write about people other than yourself.

2 Preparing the task
- Once the task has been set, you will have two hours in which to gather all your information and get ready to write your final text.
- Do your research. Authentic sources will make you sound more authoritative and will provide good vocabulary. Try searching for the information you need on German-language editions of the websites of international organisations, such as **www.greenpeace.de**.
- Remember that you are allowed to use a dictionary and reference materials at this point. Exploit this to check the genders of the words you will need to use and how to conjugate the verbs that you want to use.
- You may make notes during this period to use when completing the task for real.
- Notes should contain no more than 40 words: five bullet points with no more than eight words per bullet point – this may include conjugated verbs.
- Notes must be written on the OCR assessment writing notes form.

3 The final task
- The final task is produced under supervised control.
- You will have between 30 minutes and one hour to complete the final assessment tasks.
- You can refer only to your writing notes and a bilingual dictionary.
- You should produce the final text independently, without communicating with any other students.

4 Checking your finished work
- Make sure that you have completed all parts of the task set and that what you have written is relevant.
- Make sure that what you have written is interesting. If not, could you add colour by including more detail or by adding more of your own opinions? Try to add descriptions and include your own ideas wherever appropriate.
- Give reasons and justifications for your own views – this will give your text structure and force.
- Vary your sentence structure. Repeating the same structure too frequently can result in a rather uninteresting text. Try changing things round, for example by starting the sentence with a time expression or with a conjunction (linking word) such as *weil* (careful with the sentence order!).
- Vary your vocabulary – try to use as many different words on the topic as you can to really show off what you know.
- Read through your work several times, each time checking for a different aspect: verbs, spelling, capital letters, word order, adjectives/agreements, nouns/gender.
- Think about the number of words you have written. In order to be considered for grades C–A* you should write up to 600 words across both texts.

Pronunciation

This section helps you with your German pronunciation. Listen to the recordings and repeat the sounds you hear.

1 b, d, g

🔊 Track 13

When these letters occur at the beginning of a word, they sound much like *b* and *d* in English and the hard *g* that occurs at the beginning of the word 'golf':

billig   **D**ame   **G**ymnasium

When these consonants occur at the end of a word or in front of *s* or *t*, however, they are pronounced as follows:

b = p → e.g. *Kal**b***
d = t → e.g. *Bil**d***
g = k → e.g. *Zu**g***

Try saying the following words out loud, then listen to the recording to check your own pronunciation:

*o**b**   schrei**b**t   gesun**d**   bal**d**   Ta**g***

2 ig, ich, isch

🔊 Track 14

These three letter combinations often challenge non-native speakers of German, but it is important to pronounce them correctly to avoid misunderstandings. *Kindisch*, for example, means 'childish' in the negative sense of the word, but *kindlich* means 'childlike' in the positive sense, as in 'childlike pleasure'.

Practise these adjectives:
*wen**ig**   mögl**ich**   laun**isch***
*bill**ig**   jugendl**ich**   mod**isch***

3 ei, ie

🔊 Track 15

Although these two letter combinations are often pronounced indistinguishably in English, there is a fixed rule for how to pronounce them in German – think of the difference between *treiben* and *spielen*.

The rule is that:

– *ei* always has a long *i* sound (as in the English word 'lie')
– *ie* always has a long *ee* sound (as in the English word 'week')

It may help you to remember this if you look at the second letter of the sequence – e.g. *ei* is pronounced like the English letter *i*. Try these words:

Dienstag   Freitag
*arb**ei**ten   anb**ie**ten*
*r**ei**ten   m**ie**ten*
*L**ie**be   L**ei**d*

4 Long and short vowels

🔊 Track 16

As in English, the vowel sounds in German can be pronounced in various different ways depending on the word.

Generally, vowels that occur before two consonants, such as *tt*, *ss* or *dt* are short, and those that occur before single consonants, or before the letter *h*, are long.

Listen to the following **long vowels** and then repeat them:

m*a*g	R*a*d	s*a*gen
s*e*hr	g*e*hen	j*e*des
m*i*r	h*i*er	v*ie*l
*o*hne	w*o*hnen	*o*der
Sch*u*le	F*u*ß	z*u*

Now do the same for the following **short vowels**. Listen and repeat:

h*a*llo	*e*twas	St*a*dt
*E*ssen	T*e*nnis	schl*e*cht
s*i*ch	*i*mmer	f*i*nden
k*o*mmen	gebr*o*chen	n*o*ch
m*u*ss	M*u*tter	K*u*nst

5 Umlauts   🔊 *Track 17*

Umlauts change the way in which the vowels *o*, *a* and *u* are pronounced in German.
– *ö* is a long sound, somewhat like the *ir* sound in the English word 'bird'.
– *ü* is a short sound which sounds like a combination between a *u* and an *i*.
– *ä* sounds rather like the *e* sound in the English word 'bend'. It is generally a longer sound than the German *e*.

Repeat these words:

sch*ö*n	h*ö*her	k*ö*nnte
*ü*ber	m*ü*sste	f*ü*nf
gef*ä*hrlich	k*ä*lter	*ä*ndern

6 z and zw   🔊 *Track 18*

The German *z* sound is much harder than the English *z*. When forming it, imagine that the letter *t* comes in front of it:

Ziel	**Z**ug	**Z**immer
zwölf	**zw**ei	**zw**anzig

7 *Zungenbrecher* – tongue twisters   🔊 *Track 19*

Am Sonntag sitzt sein Sohn auf der Straße in der Stadt.
Das ist richtig aber gar nicht wichtig oder witzig.
Der Mondschein schien schon schön.
Zwischen zwei Zelten zwitschern zweiundzwanzig Zwerge.

Listening practice

Exercise 1: questions 1–5
🔊 *Track 20*

Gabi talks about her family. Read the questions. Listen to the interview and, for each question, choose the correct answer.

1 Gabi has ...
  A two brothers and two sisters. ☐
  B three brothers and one sister. ☐
  C three brothers and two sisters. ☐

2 Gabi thinks this is ...
  A dreadful – they are always fighting. ☐
  B OK – but they don't get on well. ☐
  C excellent – they never fight and are great friends. ☐

3 Gabi's brothers are ... than she is.
  A younger ☐
  B older ☐
  C two younger and one older ☐

4 ... of Gabi's brothers live/s at home.
  A None ☐
  B Some ☐
  C All ☐

5 ... of Gabi's brothers has/have children.
  A None ☐
  B Two ☐
  C All ☐

Exercise 2: questions 6–10
🔊 *Track 21*

Jan and Susi are talking about their work experience. Read the questions. Listen to the conversation and choose the correct word to end each sentence.

6 Jan found his work experience boring / tiring / dreadful.

7 Susi worked in a school / a factory / an office.

8 Jan worked in a school / a factory / an office.

9 Susi found her work experience boring / tiring / dreadful.

10 Jan / Susi / neither had a positive experience.

Exercise 3: questions 11–15
🔊 *Track 22*

Five young people discuss what they do to help protect the environment. Read the statements. Choose the correct statement for each person and write the letter in the box.

A separated rubbish
B turned off taps
C switched off electricity
D re-used plastic bags
E showered instead of taken baths
F recycled newspaper and cardboard

11	Petra	☐
12	Hans	☐
13	Meike	☐
14	Brigitte	☐
15	Klaus	☐

Exercise 4: questions 16–20   🔊 *Track 23*

A group of young people are being interviewed about their future plans. Look at the table. Then listen to the recording and fill in the table in English for each person.

16 Jochen	**Short term**	**Long term**

17 Katharina	**Short term**	**Long term**

18 Anne	**Short term**	**Long term**

19 Josef	**Short term**	**Long term**

20 Sven	**Short term**	**Long term**

Exercise 5: questions 21–25   🔊 *Track 24*

Christian talks about his brother's birthday party. Read the questions. Listen to the recording and, for each question, choose the correct answer.

21 There were ... guests at the party.
    A 50   ☐
    B 90   ☐
    C 100   ☐

22 The hotel provided ...
- **A** beef ☐
- **B** chicken ☐
- **C** lamb ☐

23 After dinner the guests ...
- **A** danced ☐
- **B** went home ☐
- **C** ate some more ☐

24 Jan was very ...
- **A** drunk ☐
- **B** sad ☐
- **C** happy ☐

25 From his parents, Jan received ...
- **A** a cheque ☐
- **B** a gold watch ☐
- **C** a car ☐

Transcripts

Exercise 1 🔊 *Track 20*

Interviewer: Gabi, erzähl mir etwas über deine Familie. Hast du Geschwister?

Gabi: Ja, ich habe drei Brüder und eine Schwester.

Interviewer: Also, eine große Familie! Wie findest du das?

Gabi: Ich finde das fantastisch. Wir streiten nie und wir sind alle Freunde.

Interviewer: Sind sie älter oder jünger als du?

Gabi: Meine Brüder sind älter, aber meine Schwester ist jünger als ich.

Interviewer: Wohnt ihr alle zu Hause?

Gabi: Nein, meine Brüder sind alle verheiratet – nur meine Schwester und ich wohnen noch zu Hause.

Interviewer: Haben deine Brüder Kinder?

Gabi: Ja, zwei haben je zwei Kinder. Ich habe zwei Nichten und zwei Neffen.

Exercise 2 🔊 *Track 21*

Jan: Ich bin so müde. Mein Arbeitspraktikum war wirklich anstrengend. Wie war denn dein Praktikum, Susi?

Susi: Ich habe in einem Büro gearbeitet – das war in Ordnung, aber ein bisschen langweilig. Wo warst du denn?

Jan: Ich musste in einer Grundschule arbeiten und den ganzen Tag Kindern helfen. Das war sehr gut, und ich fand es nie langweilig. Was hast du denn gemacht?

Susi: Ich habe viel fotokopiert und eine Menge Briefe getippt und natürlich auch viel Kaffee und Tee gekocht. Ich fand es sehr einsam. Ich konnte mit niemandem reden.

Jan: Ich konnte immer mit den Kindern reden. Ich war nie allein. Es gab immer etwas zu tun.

Susi: Da hast du aber Glück gehabt!

Exercise 3 🔊 *Track 22*

Petra: Letzte Woche habe ich viel Papier und Pappe zum Altpapiercontainer gebracht. Ich habe drei Taschen voll gehabt und es hat eine Weile gedauert, das zu entsorgen. Es ist nicht viel, aber ich tue mein Bestes für die Umwelt.

[Pause]

Hans: Gestern habe ich zum ersten Mal geduscht anstatt gebadet. Das hat viel Wasser gespart und das ist sehr gut für die Umwelt.

[Pause]

Meike: In letzter Zeit habe ich viel Energie gespart. Ich habe die Heizung heruntergedreht und ich habe das Licht ausgemacht.

[Pause]

Brigitte: Ich trenne immer den Müll. Ich habe Taschen für Papier, Glas, Dosen, Restmüll und Pappe. Ich will so viel für die Umwelt machen wie möglich.

[Pause]

Klaus: Ich finde die Umwelt sehr wichtig und ich tue, was ich kann. Meiner Meinung nach sollten wir nicht so viele Plastiktüten wegwerfen. Ich verwende immer wieder meine Tüten, und letzte Woche habe ich auch meine Mutter überredet – wir haben beim Einkaufen viele Plastiktüten wiederverwendet.

Exercise 4
Track 23

Interviewer: Jochen, was machst du nächstes Jahr?

Jochen: Ich hoffe, nächstes Jahr in die Oberstufe zu gehen. Ich will mein Abitur machen, und zwar in Englisch, Französisch und Deutsch. Danach möchte ich auf die Universität gehen. Ich möchte Fremdsprachen studieren und später in England oder Amerika arbeiten.

[Pause]

Interviewer: Und du, Katharina, was machst du nächstes Jahr?

Katharina: Also, ich will nicht studieren. Ich will eine Lehre in einem Büro machen, und dann will ich mir sobald wie möglich einen Job suchen und Geld verdienen.

[Pause]

Interviewer: Und wie sieht's bei dir aus, Anne?

Anne: Ich will nicht auf die Uni gehen, aber ich möchte auf die Hochschule gehen. Ich möchte Kunst und Design studieren, und später hoffe ich, Modedesignerin zu werden.

[Pause]

Interviewer: Und jetzt zu dir, Josef, was möchtest du mit deinem Leben machen?

Josef: Ich möchte nach der Schule sofort zur Bundeswehr gehen. Ich möchte dort eine Ausbildung als Ingenieur machen.

[Pause]

Interviewer: Und du, Sven, wie sieht's mit deiner Zukunft aus?

Sven: Ich habe vor, in einer Bank zu arbeiten. Ich muss auf die Hochschule gehen und eine Ausbildung als Bankkaufmann machen. Später möchte ich in einer internationalen Bank arbeiten.

Exercise 5
Track 24

Christian:

Letzten Samstag hatte mein Bruder Jan Geburtstag. Er wurde 18 Jahre alt, und wir haben ihm eine Party in einem Hotel gegeben. Es kamen ungefähr fünfzig Gäste.

[Pause]

Wir haben viel Wein getrunken, und das Hotel hat sich um das Essen für uns gekümmert. Es gab Hähnchen, Wurst, Salat, Brot und, natürlich, Kuchen. Es war sehr lecker.

[Pause]

Nach dem Essen haben wir eine Disko gehabt und wir haben alle viel getanzt.

[Pause]

Mein Bruder war sehr glücklich, dass seine Familie und Freunde mitgefeiert haben.

[Pause]

Er hat viele schöne Geschenke bekommen. Von unseren Eltern hat er eine goldene Armbanduhr bekommen.

Vocabulary in practice

Topic 1: Home and local area

1 Odd one out

Which is the odd one out in each group and why? For each group, add another word which *does* fit.

a	Stadt	See	Großstadt	Haupstadt	_____
b	Berge	Küste	Drogerie	Land	_____
c	Fluss	See	Stadt	Meer	_____
d	Brücke	Schwimmbad	Platz	Straße	_____
e	Krankenhaus	Boutique	Kaufhaus	Buchhandlung	_____

2 Masculine and feminine

Complete the table with the appropriate masculine/feminine equivalents.

Masculine	Feminine
der Opa	
	die Mutter
der Stiefbruder	
	die Tante
der Vetter	

3 Opposites attract

Write down the opposite of each of these adjectives.

a hübsch _____   **d** schwarz _____

b dunkel _____   **e** schlank _____

c klein _____   **f** jung _____

4 Missing consonants

Complete these forms of transport by adding the appropriate consonants.

a __ t __ a __ e__ __a__ __

b __ __ u g __ e u __

c __ä h __ e

d __u__

e __u__

f __a__ __ __ a __

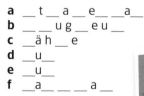

5 Places in town

Unscramble the anagrams to find the places in a town.

mDo   noiK   fohBhna   mMseuu   suaRtah
rchKie   noSdtai   ssSlohc   rTteahe   knrKasuhaen

_____   _____   _____   _____   _____

_____   _____   _____   _____   _____

Topic 2: Sport and health

6 Fruit and veg

Complete the star puzzle. Hint: all the types of fruit and vegetables are in the plural form!

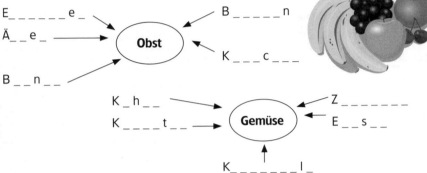

E _ _ _ _ _ _ e _

Ä _ _ e _ ⟶   Obst

B _ _ _ _ n

K _ _ _ c _ _ _

B _ _ n _ _

K _ h _ _ ⟶

K _ _ _ _ t _ _ ⟶   Gemüse

Z _ _ _ _ _ _ _

E _ _ s _ _

K _ _ _ _ _ _ _ l _

7 Illness and injury

Complete the sentences.

a Ich kann nicht sprechen. Ich habe H_____ .

b Ich habe nicht geschlafen. Ich bin so m_____ .

c Ich habe mir das B_____ gebrochen. Ich kann nicht gehen.

d Ich habe mich erkältet. Ich habe S_____ .

e Mir ist kalt, aber ich habe Fieber. Ich habe eine G_____ .

8 Unusual sports

Fill in missing the consonants and find these unusual activities.

Pa_a_ _ei_e_   _u_ _ee_ _ _i_ _e_

A _ _ _ei_ e _ _   _aja_ _ _ a _ _ _ e_

_a_ _ _ sc _ i _ _ _ _ _ _ i _ _ e _

9 Separable and inseparable verbs

Find 12 verbs from unit 2A hidden here and translate them.

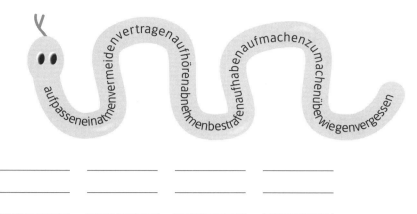

aufpasseneinatmenvermeidenvertragenaufhörenabnehmenbestrafenaufhabenaufmachenzumachenüberwiegenvergessen

_____ _____ _____ _____

_____ _____ _____ _____

_____ _____ _____ _____

10 Adjectives

Unscramble these anagrams to find 12 adjectives.

> rifhcs   kotcghe   ohr   neri   üpmefhcebdriiln   ianhäggb
> kcgüllhic   tats   hfor   tögni   eteru   eeisrwprt

Topic 3: Leisure and entertainment

11 Television and films

Fill in the missing letters to complete these types of television programme and film.

Fernsehen

S_ _ _ _ _ _p_ _ _   T_ _ _ _ _ _ _ a_
D_ _ _ _ _ _ _ _ _ _ _ _f_ _ _ _
M_ _ _ _s_ _ _ _ _ _ _   S_ _ _ t_ _ _ _ _

Kino

L_ _ _ _ s_ _ _ _   A_ _ _ _e_ _ _
S_ _ _ _ _ _ -_ _ _ _ _ _ _
H_ _ _ _ r_ _ _ _   K_ _ _ _

12 Festivals

Put these festivals in chronological order from January to December.

> Silvester   Ostern   Weihnachten   Neujahr
> Fastnacht   Pfingsten   Karneval

_____

_____

13 Past participles

What are the past participles of the following verbs?

schwimmen   gehen   lesen   hören   reiten   gewinnen   treffen   einkaufen

_____   _____   _____   _____

_____   _____   _____   _____

14 Imperfect tense

What are the imperfect stems of these same verbs?

_____   _____   _____   _____

_____   _____   _____   _____

15 Pairs

From the following ten words, make five pairs that go together.

Musik   **Sendung**   _Konzert_

Fernsehen   _Film_   **Stück**

Roman   **Theater**   **Kino**

Buch

Topic 4: Travel and the wider world

16 Countries

Unscramble these anagrams to find eight countries.

ndalrhnegiec   rnkrihcafe   nitlaei   rchieörsetr

ttnlsacdho   kamaire   nielebg   ngeornew

_____   _____   _____   _____

_____   _____   _____   _____

17 Countries and nationalities

Complete the table.

Irland		
	spanisch	
		der Russe
Frankreich		
	schweizerisch	

18 Weather adjectives

Find four pairs of opposites.

heiß	nass	wolkig	kühl
warm	sonnig	kalt	trocken

_____ – _____   _____ – _____

_____ – _____   _____ – _____

19 Environment

Find eight words to do with the environment hidden in this chain – what do they mean?

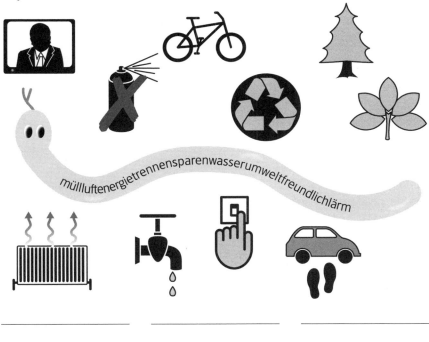

müllluftenergietrennensparenwasserumweltfreundlichlärm

_____   _____   _____

_____   _____   _____

_____   _____

20 Pairs

Find the five pairs hidden below.

Müll

sparen

Licht

schützen

trennen

Wasser

Papier

ausmachen

Umwelt

recyceln

_____ _____ _____ _____

_____ _____ _____ _____

_____ _____

Topic 5: Education and work

21 Masculine and feminine

Fill in the table with the correct male or female job title.

Male	Female
	Lehrerin
Mechaniker	
	Sekretärin
Schüler	
	Hausfrau

22 Verbs

Fill in the missing consonants to find verbs relating to school and work. Write down what each verb means.

we__ _e__   a__ __ e i _ e __   __ __ u __ ie __e __

be__ __ ehe __   __ e __ die __ e__   o__ __ a __ i __ ie__e __

_____   _____   _____

_____   _____   _____

23 School subjects

Complete the spider diagram with school subjects.

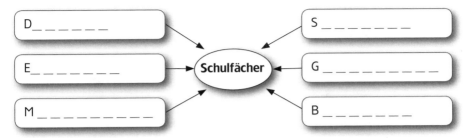

D_ _ _ _ _ _

S _ _ _ _ _ _ _ _

E_ _ _ _ _ _ _

Schulfächer

G _ _ _ _ _ _ _ _ _

M _ _ _ _ _ _ _ _ _

B _ _ _ _ _ _ _

24 Work and education

Complete the words by adding to the letter(s) given.

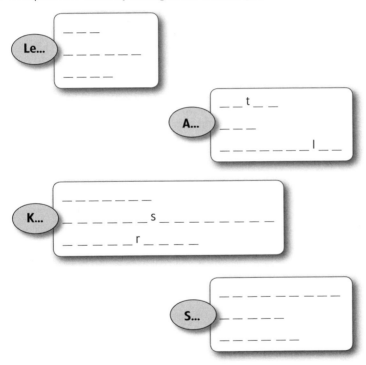

Le...

_ _ _
_ _ _ _ _ _ _
_ _ _ _

A...

_ _ t _ _ _
_ _ _ _
_ _ _ _ _ _ _ _ l _ _ _

K...

_ _ _ _ _ _ _ _
_ _ _ _ _ _ s _ _ _ _ _ _ _ _
_ _ _ _ _ r _ _ _ _ _

S...

_ _ _ _ _ _ _ _ _
_ _ _ _ _
_ _ _ _ _ _

25 *Aber, während, da, weil, und*

Complete the sentences with one of these linking words.

a Ich will die Schule verlassen, _____ ich Geld verdienen will.

b Ich möchte auf die Uni gehen, _____ meine Noten sind nicht sehr gut.

c Meine Schwester hat ihre Prüfungen bestanden _____ geht nächtes Jahr auf die Uni.

d Ich arbeite zu Hause, _____ ich viel mehr erledigen kann.

e _____ ich zu Hause bleibe, geht meine Schwester auf die Uni.

Unit 1A Mein Leben

Szenario: zum Schreiben

Students' Book page 25

Apply for a place in the *Kleiner Bruder* house.

1 You want to take part in a new reality TV series for teenagers called *Kleiner Bruder*. To apply, you need to write a paragraph for the TV company, telling them about yourself and your home life and why you think you are the ideal candidate for the programme. Brainstorm what to say for the following points. Make a note of useful vocabulary from this unit that you could use:

- who you are and where you live
- what you do at home and what your daily routine is like
- what you like about your home
- what activities you enjoy
- what your ideal house would be like
- why you want to take part in the TV programme.

- _____
- _____
- _____
- _____
- _____

2 Imagine that this is your controlled assessment and you have two hours preparation time. Brainstorm each of the points in the list above and then prepare a prompt card for this task. Include five bullet points with no more than eight words per bullet point. Include conjugated verbs if you wish.

3 Now write a draft of the application. Allow yourself 30 minutes writing time. Make sure you check your letter carefully for word order, adjectival endings and the gender of nouns.

Candidates aiming at grades C–A* should produce up to 300 words for this task.

Szenario: zum Sprechen

Students' Book page 25

Introduce yourself in a press conference.

1 Choose a famous person to play: an actor, sportsperson or politician. Prepare the questions and answers that are likely to come up in your next press conference so that you will be able to face the journalists with confidence.

2 Practise with a partner, taking turns to ask and answer questions on the points below. Use some of the filler words you have learnt in this unit if you find yourself lost for words at any time!

- where you come from
- your family
- what you usually do at home
- which is your favourite room in your house and why.

Be prepared for some unexpected questions like these:
- What are the advantages/ disadvantages of being famous?
- Do you like being famous?

Think of two more!

- _____
  _____
- _____
  _____

3 Imagine that this is your controlled assessment and you are going to prepare a prompt card for this task. Write five bullet points with no more than eight words per bullet point. Look up any words you need in the dictionary.

- _____
- _____
- _____
- _____
- _____

4 Now it's time for the press conference itself. Introduce yourself as your chosen character, remembering to mention where you come from, something about your family background and what you like doing. Record your presentation using the Record & Playback software on the OxBox. Try to speak for at least four minutes.

Aktive Grammatik

Students' Book pages 22–23

gender ■ adjective endings ■ question words

1 Nouns and articles.

Fill in the correct article and adjective endings on the following sentences.

a Sie hat ein*e* schön*e* Namen.

b D*er* klein*en* Junge ist mein Bruder.

c Ich kenne dies*e* Menschen. Das ist mein Vater.

d Wir haben ein*er* sehr intelligent*e* Sohn.

e Ich habe kein*e* Geschwister.

f Meine Schwester hat ein*en* Deutsch____ geheiratet.

g D*ie* schön*e* Frau ist meine Mutter.

h Ich habe ein*er* alt*em* Meerschweinchen.

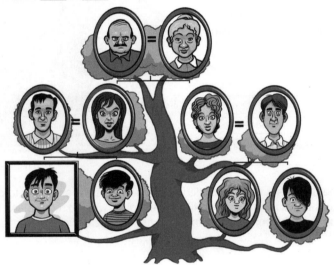

2 Interrogatives

Complete the following sentences with a question word – <u>wo?</u> wie?, <u>wer?</u>, wie <u>viele?</u>
Use each just once.

a Viele heißt deine Schwester?

b Wie Geschwister hast du?

c Wo wohnst du?

d Wer ist dein Vater?

Checklist

This chart shows the topics, skills and grammar covered in unit 1A. Use the symbols from the key to fill in the right-hand column of the table. This will help you to see what you need to spend some more time on.

☺	I know/can do this very well
😐	I'm not too sure I know/can do this
☹	I don't know/cannot do this well enough

Unit 1A Mein Leben	How confident am I?
I can	
1 give information about yourself and your family	
2 describe members of your family, friends and pets	
3 describe a typical day and daily routines and a memorable day	
4 talk about home life and relationships	
5 talk about jobs in and around the house	
Grammar	
6 use the present tense correctly	
7 use adjective endings in the accusative	
8 use personal pronouns correctly (e.g. *ich*, *du*, *Sie*)	
9 find out and use the correct gender of nouns	
10 use possessive adjectives correctly (e.g. *mein*, *dein*, *sein*)	
Skills	
11 pronounce vowel sounds correctly	
12 choose the best learning strategy for me	
13 find and correct errors	
14 rehearse in my head	
15 avoid uncomfortable silences	

Unit 1B Wohnort und Umgebung

Szenario: zum Schreiben
Students' Book page 41

Prepare a presentation about your own home town in order to win a competition to be twinned with the German town of Münster.

1 Brainstorm the most interesting buildings, places and events in your town and any green transport initiatives it has. Then write down suitable adjectives to describe them in German.

2 Choose one of the locations, events or initiatives and do some research into its background on the Internet. Imagine that this is your controlled assessment and you have two hours preparation time. Prepare a prompt card for this task. Include five bullet points with no more than eight words per bullet point. Include conjugated verbs if you wish.

- _____
- _____
- _____
- _____
- _____

3 Now write your paragraph. Allow yourself between 30 minutes and one hour. Allow yourself time to check your work carefully at the end, playing partiuclar attention to genders and adjective endings. Find pictures to illustrate your work.

Candidates aiming at grades C–A* should produce up to 300 words for this task.

Szenario: zum Sprechen

 Students' Book page 41

Meet the committee and tell them why you think your town should be chosen.

1 Write two lists: one containing questions that you think the committee are likely to ask you about your town, and one containing reasons why you think it should be chosen.

2 Now prepare your responses.
Here are some points to include:
- Why should your town be chosen?
- What is it like to live there?
- Who lives there?
- What can young people do there?
- Are there any disadvantages?
- What would you change?

Some unexpected questions:
- What do you think about the population mix (ratio of young people to old people)?
- Why is it important to have things for young people to do?
- Would you consider moving?

Think of two more!

- _____
- _____

Try to flesh out your arguments as much as possible, using plenty of adjectives, adverbs, comparatives and superlatives.

3 Imagine that this is your controlled assessment and you are going to prepare a prompt card for this task. Write five bullet points with no more than eight words per bullet point. You can include conjugated verbs.

- _____
- _____
- _____
- _____
- _____

4 Now record your presentation using the OxBox software. Try to speak for at least four minutes. When you've finished, listen to the recording and think about any aspects that you could have improved. Are there places where you could have said more or added more detail? Record a second version if you wish.

5 Swap recordings with other groups. Which group do you think had the most convincing arguments? Who do you think would have won?

Aktive Grammatik

Students' Book pages 38–39

comparatives/superlatives ■ coordinating conjunctions ■ modes of address

1 Comparatives and superlatives

Complete the sentence with the correct comparative or superlative form.

a Seine Stadt ist gut, aber meine Stadt ist _____ .

b Ich fahre schnell mit dem Rad, aber viel _____ mit dem Bus.

c Ich wohne gern in England, aber meine Mutter wohnt _____ in Schottland.

d Deine Stadt hat viele Geschäfte, seine Stadt hat mehr Geschäfte, aber meine Stadt hat _____ Geschäfte.

2 Conjunctions: coordinating (most common, e.g. *aber, oder, und*)

Which is the most appropriate conjunction in each sentence?

a Ich wohne sehr gern auf dem Land, _____ meine Schwester wohnt lieber in der Stadt.

b Meine Stadt hat viele Tennisplätze, Freibäder _____ Fußballstadien.

c Ich esse gern Pizza _____ indisches Essen.

d In meiner Stadt findet man die besten Restaurants _____ Cafés im Land.

3 You

Du, Sie or *ihr*? Which one would you use in each of the following situations?

a your local shopkeeper _____

b your cat _____

c your three best friends _____

d your mum _____

e your two brothers _____

f your teacher _____

Checklist

This chart shows the topics, skills and grammar covered in unit 1B. Use the symbols from the key to fill in the right-hand column of the table. This will help you to see what you need to spend some more time on.

☺	I know/can do this very well
☺	I'm not too sure I know/can do this
☹	I don't know/cannot do this well enough

Unit 1B Wohnort und Umgebung	How confident am I?
I can	
1 describe where I live and its advantages and disadvantages	
2 compare my town or region with a similar one in a German-speaking country	
3 find out local information in a town abroad	
4 find my way around a town or region abroad	
5 discuss aspects of travel and transport in the past, present and future	
Grammar	
6 use prepositions with accusative and dative correctly	
7 use coordinating conjunctions (e.g. *aber, oder, und*) correctly	
8 use comparative and superlative adverbs correctly	
9 use modal verbs to express feelings, abilities and obligations	
10 use the imperative to give instructions and orders	
11 recognise and use the imperfect tense of common verbs (*haben, sein* and some modals)	
Skills	
12 make clever guesses about what words mean	
13 recognise common sound–spelling links	
14 recognise 'false friends'	
15 use word families	
16 personalise vocab (e.g. sorting into categories that are personally meaningful, inventing mimes or visual images)	
17 listen in a targeted way	

Unit 2A Gesundheit und Sport

Szenario: zum Schreiben

🔍 Students' Book page 57

Plan a sporting holiday.

1 You are planning a sporting holiday to go on in the summer holidays. Brainstorm all the decisions you will need to take before planning the holiday and make a mind map of them.

2 Consider the different options for each of the things on your mind map in German and take decisions for each one.

3 Imagine that this is your controlled assessment and you have two hours preparation time. Prepare a prompt card for this task. Include five bullet points with no more than eight words per bullet point. Include conjugated verbs if you wish.

- _____
- _____
- _____
- _____
- _____

4 Write down your holiday plan, explaining where you are going and what you are going to do there. Say why you took the decisions you did and describe how you imagine a typical day on this holiday would be. Try to give as much detail as possible.

Allow yourself a maximum of one hour's writing time. Try to use expressions of time to describe what is happening at different times of day, and remember to check the word order in each sentence carefully.

Candidates aiming at grades C–A* should produce up to 300 words for this task.

Szenario: zum Sprechen

Students' Book page 57

Prepare and deliver a presentation on your sporting hero.

1 Choose the sportsperson whom you would like to nominate for sports personality of the year.

2 Start by brainstorming your ideas for what you would like to include in your presentation and how to structure it. Here are some ideas to get you started:

- Why you have chosen this hero?
- Why is he/she your hero?
- What qualities does he/she possess?
- What has he/she done recently?
- What are his/her future plans?

Some unexpected questions:

- Why is sport important?
- How does it help our daily life?
- Why do we need heroes?

Think of two more!

- _____
- _____
- _____

3 Research each of the points that you have decided to include in your presentation on the Internet. Use German search engines to find articles in German that will provide useful vocabulary.

4 Imagine that this is your controlled assessment and you are going to prepare a prompt card for this task. Write five bullet points with no more than eight words per bullet point. You can include conjugated verbs.

- _____
- _____
- _____
- _____
- _____

5 Now record your presentation using OxBox. Try to speak for at least four minutes. When you have finished, listen to your recording. Did you answer all of the questions? Could you have added more detail to any of your answers? Record a second attempt if you feel you could improve.

Aktive Grammatik

Students' Book pages 54–55

conjunctions ■ perfect tense

1 Linking words

Put the following pairs of sentences together using the conjunction given in brackets.

a Ich war jünger. Ich habe Tennis gespielt. (*als*)

_____

b Ich liebe Sport. Es ist gut für die Gesundheit. (*weil*)

_____

c Ich bin sportlich. Ich hasse Joggen. (*obwohl*)

_____

d Es kalt ist. Ich spiele Volleyball. (*wenn*)

_____

2 Perfect tense

Order these words to make complete sentences.

a habe – Sport – ich – getrieben – in der Turnhalle – mit meiner Schwester

_____

b ich – habe – letztes Jahr – gespielt – in einem Verein – Tennis – mit meinem Vater

_____

c ich – war – jünger – joggen – als – gegangen – bin – ich

_____

d sportlich – ich – sehr – einen Bruder – habe – ist – der

_____

Checklist

This chart shows the topics, skills and grammar covered in unit 2A. Use the symbols from the key to fill in the right-hand column of the table. This will help you to see what you need to spend some more time on.

☺	I know/can do this very well
☺	I'm not too sure I know/can do this
☹	I don't know/cannot do this well enough

Unit 2A Gesundheit un Sport	How confident am I?
I can	
1 talk about sports I enjoy	
2 compare sporting heroes of the past and present	
3 describe a healthy lifestyle, its benefits and how to maintain it	
4 talk about outdoor activities	
5 discuss injuries: talk about parts of the body and say where it hurts	
Grammar	
6 use the perfect tense	
7 recognise and use separable and inseparable verbs	
8 use quantifiers/intensifiers (*sehr, zu, viel, ganz, ziemlich, ein wenig, ein bisschen*)	
9 use *seit* with present tense	
10 use adverbs of time and place (*manchmal, oft, hier, dort*)	
11 use the correct word order in simple sentences	
Skills	
12 use a variety of phrases for giving opinions	
13 use description and linking words to avoid short sentences	
14 use capital letters correctly	

Unit 2B Essen und Trinken

Szenario: zum Schreiben

Students' Book page 73

Make a brochure in German for younger pupils about healthy eating.

1 Think about what healthy eating involves and make a list to be included in the brochure.
For example:
- Was bedeutet es, gesund zu essen?

2 Make up questions for the Frequently Asked Questions section of the brochure and write short replies. For example:
- Warum soll man Obst und Gemüse essen?
- Man braucht die Vitamine vom Obst und Gemüse, um gesund zu bleiben.

3 Imagine that this is your controlled assessment and you have two hours preparation time. Prepare a prompt card for this task. Include five bullet points with no more than eight words per bullet point. Include conjugated verbs if you wish.

- _____
- _____
- _____
- _____
- _____

4 Now allow yourself between 30 minutes and one hour to write a draft of your part of the brochure. Use liking words like _weil_ and _da_ to explain why eating healthily is important. Be careful with word order!

Candidates aiming at grades C–A* should produce up to 300 words for this task.

Szenario: zum Sprechen

Students' Book page 73

Prepare and deliver a presentation giving information about an eating disorder or drink problem.

1 Choose the eating/drinking problem you are going to talk about. Read through the articles in this unit and then do your own research. Search for general information about allergies and problems on the Internet, e.g. on www.wikipedia.de.

2 Prepare your presentation well. Think carefully about what you want to say. Focus on three main areas:
- descriptions of the problem
- the cause of the problem
- how to deal with it.

Imagine that this is your controlled assessment and you are going to prepare a prompt card for this task. Write five bullet points with no more than eight words per bullet point. You can include conjugated verbs.

- _____
- _____
- _____
- _____
- _____

3 Try to think of and prepare for some unexpected questions that you might be asked by your teacher or examiner. Here are some examples:
- Do you think that there is such a thing as a 'drinking culture' in Britain?
- Do you think that personal appearance is important?
- Do you think the government is right to try to control what we eat and drink so much?

Think of two more!

- _____
- _____

4 Rehearse your presentation and then record it using the OxBox software. Try to speak for at least four minutes. Once you've finished, play back your presentation to a partner and discuss which aspects you could improve.

Aktive Grammatik

Students' Book pages 70–71

accusative object pronouns ■ word order in subordinate clauses

1 **Accusative object pronouns.**
Rewrite these sentences, replacing the noun that is repeated with a pronoun (*ihn, sie* or *es*).

a Ich liebe diesen Kuchen, aber ich kann [diesen Kuchen] nicht jeden Tag essen.

_____

b Sie trinken diesen Tee selten und sie trinken [diesen Tee] nie mit Milch.

_____

c Meine Mutter kocht dasselbe Gericht jeden Freitag. Ich hasse [das Gericht]!

_____

d Das Restaurant ist sehr teuer, aber viele Leute mögen [das Restaurant] trotzdem.

_____

2 **Subordinating conjunctions and subordinate clauses**
Put the following pairs of sentences together using the conjunction in brackets (watch out for word order!).

a Ich trinke viel Wasser. Es ist gut für die Gesundheit. (*weil*)

_____

b Ich esse viele Vitamine. Mein Körper bleibt gesund. (*damit*)

_____

c Ich rauche viele Zigaretten. Das ist nicht gut für meine Lungen. (*obwohl*)

_____

d Ich esse sehr wenig. Ich will abnehmen. (*da*)

_____

Checklist

This chart shows the topics, skills and grammar covered in unit 2B. Use the symbols from the key to fill in the right-hand column of the table. This will help you to see what you need to spend some more time on.

☺	I know/can do this very well
☺	I'm not too sure I know/can do this
☹	I don't know/cannot do this well enough

Unit 2B Essen und trinken	How confident am I?
I can	
1 compare food and drink in different cultures	
2 describe my favourite foods	
3 discuss healthy and unhealthy diets, allergies and addictions	
4 shop for food	
5 eat out, order food and complain politely	
Grammar	
6 use adjective endings after definite and indefinite articles	
7 use infinitive constructions (*ohne ... zu ...*; *um ... zu ...*; verbs with *zu ...*, e.g. *beginnen, hoffen, versuchen*)	
8 use accusative object pronouns	
9 use demonstrative pronouns (*dieser* etc.)	
10 use the right adjective endings after indefinite articles and when there is no article	
Skills	
11 create my own vocab cards	
12 take good notes while listening	
13 skim read for information	
14 scan for information	
15 look for words related to others I know	

Unit 3A Freizeit

Szenario: zum Schreiben

Students' Book page 89

Write an e-mail about parties and festivals in the UK.

1 Think of a party you attended or a festival that you celebrated recently. Brainstorm the things that you did there and make a spider diagram with some ideas about the kinds of things you might want to include in your reply in German. Here are some ideas to help you get started:

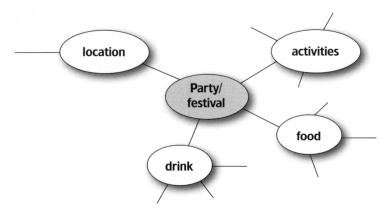

location

activities

Party/ festival

food

drink

2 Imagine that this is your controlled assessment and you have two hours preparation time. Prepare a prompt card for this task. Include five bullet points with no more than eight words per bullet point. Include conjugated verbs if you wish.

- _____
- _____
- _____
- _____
- _____

3 Now write your e-mail, giving as many details as you can.

Allow yourself between 30 minutes and one hour writing time. Use the perfect and imperfect tenses to talk about past events.

Candidates aiming at grades C–A* should produce up to 300 words for this task.

Szenario: zum Sprechen

Students' Book page 89

1 Write a questionnaire asking your classmates about how they use computers. Write at least ten questions.

Examples:
- Hast du einen Computer zu Hause?
- Was für Webseiten benutzt du am meisten?

1. _____
2. _____
3. _____
4. _____
5. _____
6. _____
7. _____
8. _____
9. _____
10. _____

2 Interview other students in your class to get their answers.

3 Prepare a short oral report about computer use in your class.

4 Try to think of and prepare for some unexpected questions that you might be asked:
- Was sind die Gefahren von Computern in der Schule?
- Was sind die Vorteile von Computern im Allgemeinen?

Think of two more!

- _____
- _____

Imagine that this is your controlled assessment and you are going to prepare a prompt card for this task. Write five bullet points with no more than eight words per bullet point. You can include conjugated verbs.

- _____
- _____
- _____
- _____
- _____

5 Now record your report on OxBox. Try to speak for at least four minutes.

Aktive Grammatik

Students' Book pages 86–87

plural forms ■ perfect tense ■ imperfect tense

1 Nouns

Complete the table with the appropriate plural forms.

	Singular	Plural
a	Kleid	
b	Hose	
c	Schuh	
d	Rock	

2 Verbs: perfect tense

Put these sentences into the perfect tense – watch out for word order!

a Ich trinke viel.

_____

b Ich gehe auf die Party.

_____

c Er isst Wurst.

_____

d Sie tanzt viel.

_____

3 Imperfect tense

Translate these sentences into German using the imperfect tense.

a I was at a friend's house. (Use *bei*)

_____

b You wanted to go shopping.

_____

c I ordered a present for my brother on the Internet.

_____

d The computer had a virus.

_____

e We went to Munich at Christmas.

_____

Checklist

This chart shows the topics, skills and grammar covered in unit 3A. Use the symbols from the key to fill in the right-hand column of the table. This will help you to see what you need to spend some more time on.

☺	I know/can do this very well
😐	I'm not too sure I know/can do this
☹	I don't know/cannot do this well enough

Unit 3A Freizeit	How confident am I?
I can	
1 plan a party: accept and decline invitations	
2 make arrangements to go out with friends	
3 go shopping for clothes and presents	
4 describe and compare festivals/special occasions in my country and another	
Grammar	
5 understand and use irregular verbs	
6 recognise and understand the future tense	
7 understand and use the imperfect tense	
8 use dative object pronouns	
Skills	
9 use my tone of voice to convey interest and enthusiasm	
10 give examples in a variety of different ways	
11 ask questions in different ways	
12 create my own vocabulary notebook organised to help your memory	
13 evaluate my guesses to judge whether they make sense in context	
14 use tone and linking words to get an idea of meaning or to guess what something means	

Unit 3B Die Medien

Szenario: zum Sprechen

Students' Book page 105

Enter a competition for the chance to interview a famous person for the TV programme called *Film heute*.

1 Research the German actors Martina Gedeck and Daniel Brühl on the Internet. Note down as much information as you can.

2 Write down what you would ask either Daniel Brühl or Martina Gedeck, and how you think they would answer your questions, in German.

Try to think of, and prepare for some unexpected questions that you might be asked by your teacher or examiner in a controlled assessment, such as:

- Why have you chosen this person?
- What have you learned from their performances?
- Why are celebrities so important?

Think of two more!

- _____
- _____

3 Imagine that this is your controlled assessment and you are going to prepare a prompt card to help you remember what to say in the interview. Write five bullet points with no more than eight words per bullet point. You can include conjugated verbs.

- _____
- _____
- _____
- _____
- _____

4 Now record your side of the interview using the Record and Playback software on the OxBox. Try to speak for at least four minutes. Remember to pay special attention to word order when asking questions.

Szenario: zum Schreiben

Students' Book page 105

Write a review of two books or two films for the school magazine of your German partner school.

1 Start by considering your choice of material. Which books or films have you read or seen recently that made a strong impression on you? Jot down the things that you particularly liked and disliked about them.

2 Now start to plan out your review. Note down information for each of the following points:
- biographical information about the director(s) and actors or the author(s)
- plot summaries
- comparisons between the two books or films
- your opinion of them both – which is your favourite?

3 Imagine that this is your controlled assessment and you have two hours preparation time. Condense your notes and prepare a prompt card for this task. Include five bullet points with no more than eight words per bullet point. Include conjugated verbs if you wish.

- _____
- _____
- _____
- _____
- _____

4 Now give yourself between 30 minutes and one hour to write a draft of your review. Try to use a variety of different phrases to express your opinions, and use the past tense to say whether your opinion of the books or films has changed over time.

Candidates aiming at grades C–A* should produce up to 300 words for this task.

Aktive Grammatik

Students' Book pages 102–103

> seit ■ impersonal verbs ■ relative pronouns

1 Time: use of *seit* with present and imperfect tense
Translate these sentences into English, paying attention to the tense.

a Seit zehn Jahren hörte ich seine Musik.

_____

b Ich will ihn seit Jahren kennenlernen.

_____

c Ich liebe ihre Bücher seit acht Jahren.

_____

d Ich spielte seit zwölf Jahren Geige.

_____

2 Verbs: impersonal (e.g. *gefallen*)
Translate these sentences into English.

a Krimis gefallen mir überhaupt nicht.

_____

b Es gefällt mir nicht, ins Kino zu gehen.

_____

3 Pronouns: relative
Translate these sentences into English.

a Kennst du den Mann, der gerade gegangen ist?

_____

b Ich liebe das Buch, das sie geschrieben hat.

_____

c Ich hasse diesen Film, den ich langweilig finde.

_____

d Ich mag nicht diese Musik, die sie immer so laut spielt.

_____

Checklist

This chart shows the topics, skills and grammar covered in unit 3B. Use the symbols from the key to fill in the right-hand column of the table. This will help you to see what you need to spend some more time on.

☺	I know/can do this very well
☻	I'm not too sure I know/can do this
☹	I don't know/cannot do this well enough

Unit 3B Die Medien	How confident am I?
I can	
1 suggest an activity or place to go out	
2 express my opinions about books, CDs and music performances	
3 give views and opinions about a well-known artist, actor or musician	
4 describe the pros and cons of different leisure activities	
5 compare my tastes and preferences now and those from when I was younger	
Grammar	
6 recognise and use weak nouns	
7 use *seit* with the imperfect tense	
8 understand and use relative pronouns	
9 recognise and use the pluperfect tense	
10 use adjectival endings after *etwas, nichts, viel, wenig, alles*	
Skills	
11 use different structures	
12 use synonyms to add colour to my writing and avoid repetition	
13 use a dictionary to find the right meaning	
14 Infer meaning from context	
15 Justify my opinions	

Unit 4A Urlaub und Austausch

Szenario: zum Schreiben

Students' Book page 121

Write a brochure about a holiday destination.

1 Choose a holiday destination to write about and do some research about it on the Internet.

2 Decide what sections to include in your brochure, e.g. Museen, Unterkunft, Nachtleben, and how you will structure it.

3 Imagine that this is your controlled assessment and you have two hours preparation time. Prepare a prompt card for this task. Include five bullet points with no more than eight words per bullet point. Include conjugated verbs if you wish.

- _____
- _____
- _____
- _____
- _____

4 Now allow yourself no more than one hour to write up your brochure. Write up each section from your plan, giving recommendations for what visitors should do. Remember to use modals to give advice, e.g.

- Man sollte unbedingt das Spielzeugmuseum besuchen.
- Man könnte eine Stadtrundfahrt machen.

Try to vary your sentence order to make it more interesting to read.

Candidates aiming at grades C–A* should produce up to 300 words for this task.

Szenario: zum Sprechen

⬥ Students' Book page 121

Plan a trip to Germany.

1 Research a tourist area in a German-speaking country on the Internet or in a travel agent's, investigating what there is to see and do there. You might want to choose an area near your partner school, a major city such as Berlin, Zurich or Vienna, or a popular holiday destination such as the Rhineland or the Swiss Alps.

2 You are planning a four-day trip to your chosen destination. Prepare a presentation about your planned trip. You should mention:
- what activities you will do
- what sights and museums you will visit
- what the nightlife will be like
- where you will stay
- how you will travel.

3 Go over the vocabulary and expressions from this unit that you will need to use, e.g. *ich habe vor*, *ich plane* etc. and try to think of and prepare for some unexpected questions that you might be asked at the end of your presentation, such as:
- Why have you chosen this destination?
- What can you learn from travelling to this area?
- Has tourism had a positive or negative effect on this area?

Think of two more!

- _____

- _____

4 Imagine that this is your controlled assessment and you are going to prepare a prompt card for this task to help you remember what to say. Write five bullet points with no more than eight words per bullet point. You can include conjugated verbs.

- _____
- _____
- _____
- _____
- _____

5 Now record your presentation on OxBox. Try to speak for at least four minutes.

Aktive Grammatik

Students' Book pages 118–119

future tense ■ conditional ■ *wenn* clauses

1 Future tense

Put these sentences into the future tense, using *werden* plus an infinitive.

a Ich fahre nach Deutschland.

_____

b Er reist nach Portugal.

_____

c Wir besuchen Freunde.

_____

d Sie fliegen nach Amerika.

_____

2 Conditional: *würde* with infinitive

Put the following sentences into the conditional.

a Ich schwimme jeden Tag.

_____

b Das tut weh.

_____

c Ich esse gern Obst.

_____

d Ich trinke nichts.

_____

3 *Wenn* clauses

Join these two sentences together using *wenn* ('if', 'whenever'). Watch out for word order changes.

a Es ist kalt in England. Ich fahre nach Spanien.

_____

b Es gibt viel Schnee. Ich fahre Ski.

_____

c Ich habe Ferien. Ich fahre ins Ausland.

_____

d Ich habe Hunger. Ich gehe ins Restaurant.

_____

Checklist

This chart shows the topics, skills and grammar covered in unit 4A. Use the symbols from the key to fill in the right-hand column of the table. This will help you to see what you need to spend some more time on.

☺	I know/can do this very well
☺	I'm not too sure I know/can do this
☹	I don't know/cannot do this well enough

Unit 4A Urlaub und Austausch	How confident am I?
I can	
1 choose and book a holiday destination	
2 make bookings and reservations, and discuss problems and complaints	
3 plan a visit to an exchange partner	
4 talk about holidays	
Grammar	
5 use *wenn* clauses with the present and future tenses	
6 use the conditional with *würde* to talk about what might happen	
Skills	
7 make recommendations	
8 express preferences and opinions in a variety of different ways	
9 give opinions of past events	
10 recognise different tenses in listening comprehensions	
11 use transcripts to develop my listening skills	

Unit 4B Die Welt und die Umwelt

Szenario: zum Schreiben

Students' Book page 137

Design an eco-outing or eco-holiday for your class.

1 Choose a destination and then brainstorm in German the things which you will need to consider when planning the trip, including travel, overnight accommodation, food (from shopping to serving), activities that are for leisure, for learning and to support the community or locality.

2 For each thing, say what you could do to make sure it is environmentally friendly. For example:

- *Ich glaube, wir sollten mit dem Flugzeug fliegen, weil das schneller geht. Wir haben nicht viel Zeit.*
- *Die Flugmeilen sind ein Problem. Meinst du, wir könnten dafür dem Woodland Trust Geld spenden, um Bäume zu pflanzen?*

3 Imagine that this is your controlled assessment and you have two hours preparation time. Prepare a prompt card that will help you to write up your plan. Include five bullet points with no more than eight words per bullet point. Include conjugated verbs if you wish.

- _____
- _____
- _____
- _____
- _____

4 Now give yourself between half an hour and an hour to write up your plan. Use modal verbs (e.g. *sollen, können*) to make suggestions. Remember to send the second verb to the end of the sentence after a modal verb.

Candidates aiming at grades C–A* should produce up to 300 words for this task.

Szenario: zum Sprechen
Students' Book page 137

Debate whether a local green area should be used for a new development.

1 Decide the basic outlines of the development – what, for whom, where, timeframe.

2 Then write a list of arguments in favour and a list of arguments against the development plan. For example:

For: *Wir brauchen mehr Häuser in dieser Stadt.*

Against: *Viele Tiere leben dort. Sie würden wahrscheinlich sterben.*

3 Focus on environmental and social aspects and what you consider to be sustainable.

4 Prepare to answer some unexpected questions such as:
- What are the benefits of protecting this area?
- What are the advantages of building on this area?

Think of two more!

- _____
- _____

5 Imagine that this is your controlled assessment and you are going to prepare a prompt card for this task. Write five bullet points with no more than eight words per bullet point. You can include conjugated verbs.

- _____
- _____
- _____
- _____
- _____

6 Now practise your arguments and record your part of the debate on OxBox. Afterwards, listen to your recording and try to think of anything that would have made your arguments even more convincing. Record a new version if you wish.

Aktive Grammatik

Students' Book pages 134–135

> **prepositions with genitive** ■ **the imperfect subjunctive** ■ **relative pronouns**

1 Prepositions: with genitive (most common, e.g. *außerhalb*, *trotz*, *während*, *wegen*)

Choose a preposition to fill each gap.

a Die Umwelt ist _____ unserer Kontrolle.

b _____ der Umwelt sollte man kein Papier wegwerfen.

c _____ des kalten Wetters sollte man die Heizung nicht so oft anmachen.

d _____ des Recyclings gibt es immer noch zu viel Müll.

2 *Hätte* or *wäre*?

Complete these sentences.

a Wenn die Umwelt wichtig _____, _____ man mehr Verständnis dafür.

b Eine saubere Umwelt _____ gut.

c Es _____ besser, wenn es keine schmutzige Luft mehr gäbe.

d Es _____ gut, wenn die ganze Welt umweltfreundlich _____

e Es _____ schade, wenn es unsere Welt nicht mehr gäbe.

3 Relative pronouns

Fill in the missing pronoun. Watch the case and gender!

a Die Umwelt, _____ uns alle betrifft, ist sehr wichtig.

b Die Leute, _____ nichts für die Umwelt machen, sind sehr umweltfeindlich.

c Ich mag jeden, _____ sich für die Umwelt bemüht.

d Das Klima, _____ sich schnell ändert, beeinflusst unsere Lebenweise.

Checklist

This chart shows the topics, skills and grammar covered in unit 4B. Use the symbols from the key to fill in the right-hand column of the table. This will help you to see what you need to spend some more time on.

☺	I know/can do this very well
☺	I'm not too sure I know/can do this
☹	I don't know/cannot do this well enough

Unit 4B Die Welt und die Umwelt	How confident am I?
I can	
1 talk about future threats and dangers to the environment	
2 discuss remedies such as conservation and recycling	
3 understand the daily routine of people living in Germany, and make comparisons with my own	
4 discuss eco-tourism	
Grammar	
5 use the future tense	
6 use the imperfect subjunctive in 'if' clauses	
7 recognise and work out the meaning of compound nouns	
8 use prepositions with the genitive (e.g. *außerhalb, statt, trotz, während, wegen*)	
Skills	
9 take notes effectively	
10 check my work to make sure my answers make sense	
11 use different strategies for remembering tenses	

Unit 5A Schule und Taschengeld
Szenario: zum Schreiben

Students' Book page 153

Decide on the priorities of the school council.

1 Make a list in German of what you think the main issues faced by your school are, e.g.
- *Gebäude zu klein*
- *Keine Recyclingcontainer*

2 Decide what changes you would like to see take place in your school and why you want those changes. Your list might include some of the following:
- timetabling
- homework
- subjects
- the school day
- school facilities
- opportunities for events.

3 Imagine that this is your controlled assessment and you have two hours preparation time. Prepare a prompt card for this task. Include five bullet points with no more than eight words per bullet point. Include conjugated verbs if you wish.

- _____
- _____
- _____
- _____
- _____

4 Now write up an agenda for your school council, listing your priorities and explaining why they are important, using *weil*. Allow yourself between 30 minutes and one hour to write up the task. Remember to check your word order carefully after conjunctions.

Candidates aiming at grades C–A* should produce up to 300 words for this task.

Szenario: zum Sprechen

Students' Book page 153

The ideal part-time job

1 Decide what you think the perfect part-time job would be for teenagers who are still at school and so need time for homework and school-based activities.

2 Write notes in German on the following aspects of the job:
- where the job is
- what the hours are
- what tasks are involved
- pay
- opportunities for the future
- other significant aspects.

3 Prepare to give a presentation in German about the job to convince potential students to apply for it. Emphasise all the advantages and try to be as persuasive as possible.

Make sure you are ready to answer some unexpected questions such as these:
- Why is it important to have a job?
- What are the dangers of doing nothing?

Think of two more!

- _____
- _____

4 Imagine that this is your controlled assessment and you are going to prepare a prompt card for this task. Write five bullet points with no more than eight words per bullet point. You can include conjugated verbs.

- _____
- _____
- _____
- _____
- _____

5 Rehearse your presentation and then record it on OxBox. Try to speak for at least four minutes. Use imperatives (orders) and superlatives (e.g. *der beste Job*) to make your presentation as convincing as possible.

eflexive verbs which take the accusative and dative ■ *weil* and *um...zu*

1 Reflexive verbs
Fill in the correct reflexive pronoun in each of the following sentences.

a Ich interessiere _____ sehr für die Umwelt.

b Wir erinnern _____ oft an eine Zeit ohne solche Umweltprobleme.

c Sie (*they*) interessieren _____ überhaupt nicht für solche Themen.

d Warum habt ihr _____ nicht dafür interessiert?

2 Reflexive pronouns in the dative
Fill in the correct pronoun in each sentence.

a Es tut _____ Leid. (*him*)

b Es gefällt _____ . (*her*)

c Das macht _____ keinen Spaß. (*me*)

d Es geht _____ auf die Nerven. (*us*)

e Gefällt es _____? (*you informal*)

3 Revision of *weil* and *um...zu*.
Put the words in the correct order to make sentences.

a Nebenjob weil Taschengeld brauche ich habe mehr ich einen

_____

b Noten bekommen zu wir fleißig arbeiten sehr um gute

_____

c Umwelt um schützen wir Schule trennen den Müll in zu unserer die

_____

d werden Maria Uni will Lehrerin die gehen auf sie möchte weil

_____

e Berufsschule möchte weil Bernd die Automechaniker auf er werden geht

_____

Checklist

This chart shows the topics, skills and grammar covered in unit 5A. Use the symbols from the key to fill in the right-hand column of the table. This will help you to see what you need to spend some more time on.

☺	I know/can do this very well
☺	I'm not too sure I know/can do this
☹	I don't know/cannot do this well enough

Unit 5A Schule und Taschengeld	How confident am I?
I can	
1 give my opinions about school and school subjects	
2 compare the subjects I study	
3 compare my school life here with that in a German-speaking country	
4 talk about money and finding part-time jobs	
5 discuss the pros and cons of young people having part-time jobs	
Grammar	
6 use reflexive pronouns with the accusative and dative	
7 understand and use weak nouns	
8 use conjunctions effectively (*aber, weil, während*)	
9 use infinitive constructions (*um ... zu, ohne ...zu* etc.)	
Skills	
10 give answers by adapting the question	
11 anticipate questions by context/common sense	
12 turn statements into questions to avoid forgotten questions words	
13 embellish the truth in order to show off my German	
14 focus on key details needed when answering a question	

Unit 5B Arbeit und Zukunftspläne

Szenario: zum Sprechen
Students' Book page 169

Debate: Is work experience a waste of time?

1 To prepare for the debate, brainstorm the different aspects of work experience and make a mind map:

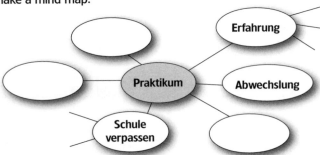

Erfahrung

Praktikum

Abwechslung

Schule verpassen

2 Make a list in German of the advantages and disadvantages of doing work experience. What is your conclusion: are you in favour or against?

Vorteile	Nachteile
Man kriegt Erfahrung	Man bekommt nur langweilige Aufgaben

3 Imagine that this is your controlled assessment and you are going to prepare a prompt card that will help you to remember the arguments you want to present. Write five bullet points with no more than eight words per bullet point. You can include conjugated verbs.

4 Prepare to respond to unexpected questions that your teacher or examiner might ask you, such as:

- _____
- _____
- _____
- _____
- _____

- Why do you think work experience is compulsory?
- What can we learn from working with other people?

Think of two more!

- _____
- _____

5 Practise for the debate by recording your side of the argument on OxBox. Try to speak for at least four minutes.

Szenario: zum Schreiben

Students' Book page 169

Tell the best work experience story.

1 Think of a work experience placement that you have been on, or think of an imaginary work experience placement to write about. Now brainstorm the details of an attention-grabbing story about what happened during the placement. Include:
   • where the placement was
   • when it happened
   • who you were working for
   • how long the placement was
   • what happened (try to make this part as funny or dramatic as possible!).

2 Imagine that this is your controlled assessment and you have two hours preparation time. Prepare a prompt card that will help you to remember the details of the story you want to write. Include five bullet points with no more than eight words per bullet point. Include conjugated verbs if you wish.

   • _____
   • _____
   • _____
   • _____
   • _____

3 Now allow yourself up to one hour to write a draft of your story. To maximise your marks, try to use as many different tenses as possible (especially the perfect and imperfect to describe what happened) and use a variety of different sentence structures.

   Candidates aiming at grades C–A* should produce up to 300 words for this task.

Aktive Grammatik

Students' Book pages 166–167

1 Grammar checklist quiz

a What is a noun?

_____

b What are the three genders in German?

_____

c What are the four cases?

_____

d What is an adjective?

_____

e How many adjectival endings are there?

_____

f What is a verb?

_____

g What is the pattern for regular verb endings in the present tense?

_____

h How do you form the perfect tense in German?

_____

i How do you form the past participle of a regular verb?

_____

j How do you form the future tense?

_____

k What are the six modal verbs?

_____

l What are the different ways of saying 'you'?

_____

m Where does the verb normally appear in a sentence?

_____

n What do you understand by time–manner–place?

_____

o What do _wenn, dass_ and _weil_ do to the order of a sentence?

_____

p What does _um ... zu_ mean?

_____

q Can you name the most common question words?

_____

r Can you name five separable verbs?

s What happens to separable verbs in the present tense?

t What happens to separable verbs in the perfect tense?

Checklist

This chart shows the topics, skills and grammar covered in unit 5A. Use the symbols from the key to fill in the right-hand column of the table. This will help you to see what you need to spend some more time on.

☺	I know/can do this very well
☺	I'm not too sure I know/can do this
☹	I don't know/cannot do this well enough

Unit 5B Arbeit und Zukunftspläne	How confident am I?
I can	
1 choose and apply for a work experience placement	
2 discuss the benefits and disadvantages of work experience	
3 talk about further education and types of career	
4 talk about the advantages and disadvantages of working abroad	
5 write a CV and apply for a job	
Grammar	
6 use different tenses (past, present, future and conditional) in writing and speech	
7 use the correct word order in simple and more complex sentences	
8 use the appropriate form of address (*du, ihr* or *Sie*) when talking to different people	
Skills	
9 use idiomatic phrases and avoid word-for-word translations	
10 understand the conventions of formal and informal writing	
11 work out meaning from context/common sense	
12 write longer sentences using linking words and by giving more details	
13 use a checklist for proofreading work	

Oxford University Press

Great Clarendon Street, Oxford OX2 6DP

Oxford University Press is a department of the University of Oxford. It furthers
the University's objective of excellence in research, scholarship, and education
by publishing worldwide in

Oxford New York

Auckland Cape Town Dar es Salaam Hong Kong Karachi Kuala Lumpur
Madrid Melbourne Mexico City Nairobi New Delhi Shanghai Taipei Toronto

With offices in

Argentina Austria Brazil Chile Czech Republic France Greece Guatemala
Hungary Italy Japan Poland Portugal Singapore South Korea Switzerland
Thailand Turkey Ukraine Vietnam

Oxford is a registered trade mark of Oxford University Press in the UK and in
certain other countries

British Library Cataloguing in Publication Data

Data available

ISBN-13: 978 0 19 915495 1

10 9 8 7 6 5 4 3 2 1

Printed in Great Britain by Ashford Colour Press Ltd.

Paper used in the production of this book is a natural, recyclable product made
from wood grown in sustainable forests. The manufacturing process conforms
to the environmental regulations of the country of origin.

Acknowledgements
The publishers would like to thank the following for permission to reproduce
photographs: 37a OUP, 41a OUP, 45a OUP.

All illustrations by Kessia Beverley Smith, Phillip Burrows, Stefan Chabluk,
Moreno Chiacchiera, Mark Draisey, Mark Duffin, Fenton, Bill Greenhead, John
Hallett, Bill Houston, Richard Jones, Tim Kahane/www.hardwickstudios.com,
Mike Lacey, Lee Nicholls/www.hardwickstudios.com, Pulsar Studio, Andy Robb,
Simon Tegg, Theresa Tibbetts, Laszlo Veres.

Cover photo Erik Isakson/Getty

The author and publishers would like to thank the following people for their
help and advice: Robert Anderson; Marion Dill; Helen Smith; Colette Thomson
and Andrew Garratt (Footstep Productions).

Every effort has been made to contact copyright holders of material reproduced
in this work. If notified, the publishers will be pleased to rectify any errors or
omissions at the earliest opportunity.